Original title:
Chosen Chaos

Copyright © 2024 Creative Arts Management OÜ
All rights reserved.

Author: Miriam Kensington
ISBN HARDBACK: 978-9916-90-588-3
ISBN PAPERBACK: 978-9916-90-589-0

Embrace the Unraveled

Threads of life pull and fray,
In the twilight where shadows play.
Let go of what binds you tight,
And dance through the endless night.

Woven tales of joy and sorrow,
Flickering dreams of tomorrow.
In chaos, find your hidden grace,
And smile in this vast space.

The tangled path leads you home,
Into the unknown, you freely roam.
With each step, embrace the air,
Unraveled, yet we find repair.

The Melody of the Messy

Life is a song, full of strife,
Each note a piece of fragile life.
Harmony found in disarray,
Listen closely, hear what they say.

Rhythms clash, yet they can blend,
Messy paths bend without end.
In discord, we find the tune,
A melody beneath the moon.

With every stumble, find the beat,
In shattered moments, rise to greet.
Celebrate the flaws, don't fret,
In the messy, joy is met.

The Confluence of Chaos

Rivers collide in a wild dance,
Sparks ignite with fleeting chance.
In chaos, stories intertwine,
Fate's design, a grand outline.

Waves crashing on shores of time,
Each moment a fleeting rhyme.
Beneath the tempest, seeds of change,
A world reborn, profound and strange.

Navigate through the turbulent flow,
Trust the path, and let it show.
In this maelstrom, find your way,
Embrace the chaos, come what may.

The Embrace of Entropy

In the dance of time, we spin,
Where order fades, and chaos begins.
Embrace the fall of perfect lines,
The beauty found where tension twines.

Stars collide in the vast unknown,
In every fracture, seeds are sown.
In wild disorder, life ignites,
Through abandoned plans, our spirit fights.

Let go of the need to control,
In entropy, discover your soul.
Within the chaos, find your art,
A masterpiece crafted from the heart.

Whirlwinds of Fortune

In the dance of chance we spin,
Fortunes rise and fortunes thin.
Whispers of fate in the breeze,
Guide us forward with playful ease.

A tempest roars, a fortune sways,
Weaving dreams through tangled ways.
In shadows cast by hopes unbound,
The echoes of the lost are found.

With every twist, a story's hurled,
Secrets hidden in a swirling world.
To ride the gusts that fate will send,
Is to embrace the wind as friend.

So let us leap into the gale,
Trusting fortune will prevail.
For in the whirl, our spirits soar,
In every turn, we seek for more.

Rhapsody in Ruins

In shadows deep where echoes dwell,
The remnants sing their broken spell.
A melody of what once was,
In silence lost, beneath the buzz.

The crumbling walls tell tales of yore,
Of laughter shared and love no more.
Each brick a note in mournful song,
A rhapsody where hearts belong.

Fragments fall like autumn leaves,
Beauty found in what deceives.
In every crack and crevice bare,
Lies the essence of memories rare.

The ruins hum a lullaby,
A gentle whisper, a soft sigh.
From decay, new life shall bloom,
In every shadow, dispel the gloom.

Elysium in Entropy

Amidst the chaos, beauty thrives,
In shattered dreams, a spark survives.
Entropy's dance, a wild embrace,
Rebirth found in every trace.

Whispers of nature in twilight speak,
Life from ruins, strong yet meek.
A paradox, where chaos reigns,
Elysium blooms from tangled chains.

Petals fall like fleeting time,
In disarray, a rhythm's rhyme.
From ashes rise the dreams we dream,
In entropy's heart, we find our beam.

So in the storm, let us rejoice,
In every moment, heed our voice.
For from the wreckage, we shall find,
An Elysium in every mind.

The Gift of Disruption

In quiet seams, a ripple grows,
The world awakens, and chaos flows.
Disruption sings a vibrant tune,
In every dawn, the old must swoon.

A breaking wave, the status shatters,
In vulnerability, the spirit scatters.
Yet in the space where things unwind,
New paths emerge for hearts that bind.

Stars align in unexpected ways,
Beauty born from disarray.
The gift of change, a fearless leap,
In every fracture, treasures keep.

So let us dance in the unknown,
Embrace the gift that's come to own.
In disruption's wake, we shall find,
A brighter world, a bolder mind.

Revelations in the Reckless

In the shadow's clutch we find,
Whispers of truths long left behind.
Bold steps taken, hearts collide,
Reckless dreams we cannot hide.

Fleeting moments paint the night,
Lost in chaos, seeking light.
With every fall, we learn to rise,
Revealing wisdom in disguise.

A dance of fate, a silent scream,
In every folly, we redeem.
The thrill of risk, the lure of chance,
Life unfolds in reckless dance.

With open hearts, we dare to roam,
In every venture, we find home.
Amidst the storm, our fears dissolve,
In reckless truths, our souls evolve.

The Tangle of Time

Winding pathways through the haze,
Moments lost in endless maze.
Ticking clocks and fading light,
Time entwines both day and night.

Threads of yesterday pull tight,
Yesterday's shadows, future's flight.
Every choice a ripple flows,
In tangled webs, the mystery grows.

Echoes call from distant lands,
Grasping softly with our hands.
The dance of ages, slow yet swift,
In the tangle, we find our gift.

Turning leaves, a constant change,
Moments drift, yet feel so strange.
In each heartbeat, stories chime,
We weave our lives in tangle of time.

Echoes of Euphoria

High above the world we soar,
In fleeting seconds, we explore.
Electric laughter fills the air,
Ephemeral joys that we all share.

With every pulse, our spirits rise,
Chasing visions painted skies.
When laughter fades, what remains?
Echoes soft in joyous strains.

A teardrop falls, but joy resides,
Within the heart, where love abides.
In unity, we find our sound,
In echoes deep, the bliss unbound.

Moments captured, fleeting grace,
In every hug, a warm embrace.
Through whispered dreams, we leap and twirl,
In echoes of this wondrous whirl.

Chasing the Chaotic Muse

On winding roads, we chase the spark,
In chaos dwells the vital arc.
Brush strokes wild on canvas bright,
Chasing visions in the night.

A whirlwind dance of thought and style,
Lost in rhythms, bask in the while.
With every twist, a story spun,
The path of chaos, the artist's run.

In scattered pages, dreams ignite,
The muse awakens, pure delight.
Through storms we venture, hearts ablaze,
In disarray, we find our ways.

Each fleeting moment, a vibrant hue,
In chaotic journeys, life feels new.
Through every stumble, we learn to choose,
Forever chasing the chaotic muse.

Fireflies in a Storm

In the dark, they flicker bright,
Guiding hearts through the night.
Dance of light in heavy rain,
Whispers soft, ease the pain.

Storm clouds rumble, winds do wail,
Yet beneath, fireflies prevail.
A spark of hope amidst the dread,
Dreams ignited, fears shed.

Nature's lanterns, small yet bold,
Silent stories, softly told.
In the chaos, find your glow,
Let your inner fire show.

Through the tempest, keep the flame,
Eternal light, never the same.
Together we forge through the gloom,
Fireflies' dance, life's sweet bloom.

Amidst the Clamor of Choices

In a world where voices clash,
Paths diverge, moments flash.
Whispers pull from every side,
In the noise, we must abide.

Decisions loom like towering trees,
Branches swaying in the breeze.
Heartbeats echo, minds entwine,
Finding clarity in the sign.

Each option glimmers with its lure,
Yet only one path feels so pure.
Amidst the chaos, seek the calm,
Trust the journey, find the balm.

With each choice, a tale unfolds,
A mosaic of dreams retold.
In the dance of fate and chance,
Embrace the ride, join the dance.

The Canvas of Dissonance

Strokes of color, bright and bold,
Amidst the chaos, stories told.
Harmony mingles with discord's sound,
In this dance, art is found.

Splattered paint, a vivid scene,
Rushing waves and spaces between.
Each layer adds a tale of strife,
A reflection of our complex life.

Cacophony in every hue,
A masterpiece waiting to break through.
In dissonance, find the grace,
In every nuance, a sacred space.

Every clash sings a song,
In this world where we belong.
The canvas blooms in vibrant light,
Chaos crafted, pure delight.

Laughter in the Face of Uncertainty

In shadowed halls where doubts reside,
Laughter echoes, bright and wide.
Through the fog of what's unknown,
Joyful hearts are freely sown.

Life's riddles twist and twine,
Find the humor in the line.
Each misstep, a chance to smile,
Wandering with a playful style.

Caught between the blaze and chill,
Laughter rises, softens will.
In uncertainty, joy holds sway,
Light and laughter lead the way.

Gather close, let your fears blend,
In this space, let your heart mend.
With laughter's spark, we pave the road,
Finding light in every load.

Unraveled Threads of Fate

In shadows deep, where secrets lie,
Hope whispers soft, the heart's quiet sigh.
Each step we take, a thread unwound,
In the tapestry of life, lost and found.

Stars align, then soon collide,
Paths entwined, we cannot hide.
Fate's slender hands weave night and day,
The beauty forged from choices made away.

Winds of change blow fierce and bold,
Stories waiting, yet untold.
With every twist and turn, we face,
In tangled dreams, we find our place.

Beneath the veil, the truth may gleam,
As we navigate this fragile dream.
Through threads unraveled, we shall chase,
The fabric of our fleeting grace.

Anarchy's Soft Embrace

Whispers dance in the dark of night,
Rebels gather, hearts set alight.
Freedom calls in a silken tone,
In chaos born, we feel at home.

The rules laid down begin to bend,
With every voice, a chance to mend.
Exiled hopes take flight once more,
In the space between, we explore.

Anarchy's lullaby sings sweet,
In disarray, our spirits meet.
With open arms, we break the mold,
A journey shared, our stories told.

In the noise, a calming grace,
Embraced by dreams, we find our place.
Chaos softens, leads us to see,
In this wild dance, we learn to be.

The Melody of Misfits

In corners dim, where outcasts play,
A symphony born of night and day.
Each note a story, each chord a tear,
In harmony's grip, we've nothing to fear.

Canvas bright with colors bold,
Misfits rise, defying the cold.
Through laughter shared, and sorrows sung,
A melody vibrant, forever young.

Together we weave our joyful tune,
Under starlit skies, beneath the moon.
Unlikely friends, a tapestry spun,
In every heart, a fire begun.

Though the world may often divide,
In unity's song, we shall abide.
The melody of misfits shall soar,
In brokenness, we find our core.

When Order Meets the Unexpected

In measured steps, we tread the line,
Order reigns with a steady spine.
But just beyond the rigid plan,
Lies a spark that ignites the span.

Whispers of change swirl in the air,
Unexpected turns, we hardly prepare.
Life's rich tapestry begins to fray,
In chaos found, new paths display.

The clock ticks loud, but moments pause,
In stillness, we find our own cause.
When balance shifts and norms decay,
Innovation blooms in bright array.

So dance with fate, let structures bend,
Embrace the wild, let patterns end.
For when order meets the bold surprise,
New worlds awaken, and dreams arise.

Harmonies of the Unforeseen

In shadows where the secrets play,
A whisper calls the dawn to stay.
Unseen paths begin to twist,
In melodies that can't be missed.

The stars align in perfect rhyme,
As dreams awaken, weaving time.
With every note, the heart will soar,
In harmonies forever more.

Through trials faced and laughter shared,
For every moment, we have dared.
With open hearts, we chase the light,
In tunes of hope that feel so right.

So let the music guide our feet,
In unforeseen, where souls can meet.
Together we will sing the tune,
A dance beneath the silver moon.

A Tapestry of Woven Whimsy

In threads of gold, the stories gleam,
A dreamer's eye creates the seam.
With laughter wrapped in colors bright,
We stitch our hopes in sheer delight.

The gentle sway of playful threads,
In whimsical forms, our spirit spreads.
Each laugh a knot, each tear a hue,
A tapestry that feels so true.

Crafting memories, we intertwine,
As hearts collide, our fates align.
With every loop and every spin,
The joy of life begins within.

So let us weave with love and cheer,
A masterpiece that draws us near.
In every pattern, dreams unveiled,
Our woven whimsy will prevail.

Crescendo of the Unorthodox

In echoes bold, a sound breaks free,
A symphony of you and me.
With every clash, a pulse ignites,
In unorthodox, we find new heights.

The rhythm shifts, the tempo sways,
Embracing strange in myriad ways.
With every note, we redefine,
The boundaries of the grand design.

In vibrant hues, the discord sings,
We dance on air with vibrant wings.
The world outside fades to a blur,
In whispers soft, our spirits stir.

So let the music play its part,
In crescendos born from daring heart.
Together we will rise and soar,
In unorthodox, forevermore.

The Unscripted Journey

With no script held, we roam the wild,
Heart open wide, forever a child.
Each step we take, a tale unfolds,
In ventures bold, our spirit holds.

Through tangled paths and skies unknown,
In whispered dreams, our courage grown.
Adventure calls in vibrant hues,
The journey's ours, a life to choose.

Every twist and turn reveals,
The magic hidden in what feels.
With laughter sharing burdens light,
In unscripted it feels so right.

So let us wander, hand in hand,
Creating memories unplanned.
In every day, a story's spun,
The unscripted journey has begun.

The Exquisite Mess

Colors splatter on the ground,
Chaos reigns, yet beauty found.
A canvas rich in shades of pain,
Life's creation, wild and untamed.

Broken pieces form a tale,
Whispers echo, soft and pale.
A dance of dreams in disarray,
In every flaw, the heart's ballet.

Amidst the wreckage, hope does bloom,
From tangled threads, we find our room.
A mess transformed to art divine,
In every shadow, light will shine.

So let the chaos have its sway,
In every struggle, find your way.
For in the mess, our truths confess,
Life's exquisite, loving mess.

Threads of Turmoil

Life unwinds, a tangled skein,
Threads of joy and threads of pain.
Each strand tells a story deep,
In turmoil's grasp, the heart must leap.

A tapestry of doubts and dreams,
Woven tightly, bursting seams.
Stitch by stitch, we mend the fray,
Finding strength in disarray.

Through storms of fear, the fibers pull,
In every struggle, the heart feels full.
Tied together, we stand tall,
Resilience rises, breaking fall.

With every tear, a lesson learned,
In every fire, a heart that burned.
Threads of turmoil, harsh yet true,
From chaos, we are born anew.

Feast of Fractures

Gather 'round this broken tale,
Where laughter echoes, spirits sail.
A banquet laid with shards of glass,
In fractured moments, memories pass.

Each slice reveals a hidden truth,
In autumn's chill, we seek our youth.
Taste the joy, indulge the pain,
In every tear, the love remains.

So raise a glass to what has been,
Celebrate the loss, and win within.
For every crack is part of us,
In feast of fractures, we find trust.

From shattered dreams, a new path grows,
A symphony of highs and lows.
In every break, a song's refrained,
Amidst the feast, hope is gained.

Resilience in Reverberation

Echoes linger in the air,
Resilience blooms, a silent prayer.
Through trials faced, a spirit strong,
In every heartbeat, the pulse of song.

Waves of doubt may crash and break,
But from each fall, a path we make.
In whispered winds, our courage lies,
Rising high like flares in skies.

Harmony found in the disharmony,
In every struggle, a symphony.
We bend but do not break apart,
For in our scars, we find our art.

So let the echoes shape our way,
Through darkened nights to light of day.
Resilience finds its voice, its sound,
In reverberation, hope is found.

The Cornerstone of Confusion

In shadows deep, where whispers play,
Thoughts collide, then drift away.
A puzzle formed without an end,
Lost in mazes, minds descend.

Fleeting glimpses, truth obscured,
Memories twist, the heart feels stirred.
In chaos soft, we seek the light,
Yet questions linger through the night.

The Lullaby of Disorder

Softly sung, the chaos hums,
In tangled dreams, the silence comes.
A cradle rocked by doubts that soar,
Melodies of what was before.

Whispers swirl in nightly air,
A soothing balm for souls laid bare.
In gentle tones, disorder sways,
While hopes and fears weave through the haze.

Finding Clarity in the Confusion

Through tangled thoughts, I walk the road,
Seeking paths where dreams are sowed.
In paradox, the truth will gleam,
A silent promise in the stream.

With every step, the fog lifts slow,
Revealing what I thought I'd know.
In moments brief, the vision clears,
Unraveling doubts, confronting fears.

The Joyride of Uncertainty

Wheels spinning fast on roads unknown,
A thrill that chills, yet feels like home.
In reckless dance, the heart takes flight,
Embracing all that feels so right.

With laughter loud and spirit free,
Each twist and turn, a jubilee.
Through leaps of faith, we learn to steer,
In joyride's grip, we shed our fear.

Whimsy in Whirlwinds

In a dance of delight, the breezes play,
Colors twirl wildly, brightening the day.
Joyful whispers ride on the gusts so sweet,
Nature's laughter echoes, a whimsical treat.

Clouds giggle softly, drifting on high,
Kites soar and spin, painting the sky.
A child chases shadows, skipping along,
As chaos embraces a whimsical song.

Laughter and flutter, bright as a flame,
Every twist in the air, never the same.
With every turn, a new story unfolds,
Whimsy in whirlwinds, a joy to behold.

The Melancholy of Mayhem

In shadows we linger, where silence looms,
Flashes of chaos dance in dark rooms.
The heart aches softly, like rain on bare ground,
In whispers of mayhem, lost dreams can be found.

Fragments of laughter, now distant and frail,
Memories linger, like a bittersweet trail.
Colors fade slowly, a palette of gray,
In the melancholy, we drift and sway.

Yet through the sorrow, a flicker may spark,
Life's strange symphony, with light in the dark.
Hope may arise when least expected,
Amidst the mayhem, a soul resurrected.

Symphony of the Unexpected

Notes of surprise, like raindrops that fall,
A melody echoes, enchanting us all.
In the chaos of life, we uncover the score,
A symphony plays, opening the door.

Each twist in the path, a rhythm so bold,
Uncharted adventures, waiting to unfold.
Dissonance fades, harmony draws near,
In unexpected moments, joy becomes clear.

The clashing of days, a cacophony bright,
Starlight and shadows unite in the night.
A dance of beginnings, a brand new refrain,
In the symphony's heart, we find love's sweet gain.

The Unexpected Harmony

When storms surge and clash, a strange peace can grow,
In the heart of the tempest, we learn to let go.
Unexpected harmony weaves through the fray,
A melody blooms where chaos holds sway.

Soothing the wild with a soft serenade,
Each note a reminder of dreams yet to fade.
In the laughter of thunder, the song intertwines,
Creating a rhythm where darkness aligns.

With whispers of breezes that tickle the trees,
We find in the noise a gentle reprise.
Together we stand, as the world spins around,
In unexpected harmony, true beauty is found.

The Dance of Disarray

In shadows cast by dim-lit night,
A waltz unfolds without a fright.
The steps are lost, yet hearts still soar,
In chaos found, we crave for more.

With every turn, the world spins free,
Unraveled threads, a tapestry.
In disarray, we find our song,
A melody where we belong.

As laughter echoes, fears dissolve,
In tangled paths, our hearts evolve.
Embracing flaws, we leap and prance,
In the wild blur, we learn to dance.

Among the stars, we weave our fate,
In every twist, we love, we wait.
The dance of life, a vibrant sway,
In sweet disarray, we find our way.

Harmony in Haphazardness

The sun peeks through the breaks of dawn,
Amongst the chaos, dreams are drawn.
A world of clutter, colors burst,
In haphazardness, we quench our thirst.

Notes collide like waves on shore,
Each discord blooms to something more.
In tangled strings, a harmony,
In every mess, a reverie.

With open arms, we greet the stir,
In wildness found, we sense a blur.
The melody of life, askew,
Creates a path for hearts so true.

So dance, dear souls, amidst the fray,
In vibrant hues, let fears decay.
For in this tangle, bond and blend,
We find the beauty that will mend.

Fractured Symphony

A fractured tune, a broken string,
Yet still a note that yearns to sing.
In shards of sound, our spirits rise,
A symphony beneath the skies.

Each clash of chords, a tale unfolds,
In every pause, the heart beholds.
A canvas strewn with shattered light,
In every wrong, we find what's right.

The tempo shifts, the rhythm sways,
In lost refrain, we find our ways.
With tender hands, we play the keys,
In fractured notes, we find the peace.

Resilient harmony ignites,
In echoes deep, the heart alights.
Through brokenness, a strength we find,
In fractured symphony, we're entwined.

Embracing the Tumult

In whirling winds, we find our ground,
In every storm, new life is found.
The tempest roars, yet we stand tall,
Embracing tumult, we won't fall.

Through raging waves, we surf the tide,
In chaos fierce, our hearts collide.
With hands outstretched, we greet the waves,
Within the tumult, the brave heart saves.

A symphony of thunder cracks,
Yet in that sound, the courage stacks.
With every crash, we learn to soar,
In chaos' heart, we seek for more.

So let the wild winds freely blow,
In paths unknown, our spirits grow.
With every turn, embrace the fight,
In tumult's arms, we find the light.

Whispers of Wild Conformity

In shadows where the wild things roam,
Nature whispers secrets, far from home.
A dance of leaves in the evening breeze,
Echoes of freedom that aim to please.

Each heartbeat matches the rustling ground,
In tangled woods, serenity is found.
The chains of order slip softly away,
Inviting the wild to come out and play.

A song of chaos, in darkness it sings,
Embracing the beauty that wildness brings.
Let not the norms shackle our delight,
For in wild whispers, we reclaim the night.

Symphony of Shattered Order

In fragments of silence, chaos takes flight,
Each note of disarray paints the night.
A melody born from the fissures of time,
Where harmony struggles to find its rhyme.

Disorder dances on the edge of the sane,
With every step, it breaks from the chain.
The strings of the past are frayed and worn,
In this symphony, new paths are born.

Listen closely as the clamor arises,
A clash of the worlds, a dance that surprises.
In shattered remains, we find our refrain,
In discordant beauty, we relish the pain.

Serenade of the Unruly Heart

A heart unleashed, unbound from the cage,
Beating to rhythms that set the stage.
In whispers of love, a fire ignites,
Embracing the chaos, chasing the nights.

With every pulse, a story is spun,
An anthem of dreams that can never be done.
The unruly spirit yearns to be free,
In melodies woven like roots of a tree.

Each note a rebellion, each chord a sigh,
A serenade cast to the stars in the sky.
For in wild abandon, our spirits will soar,
Celebrating the heart that forever wants more.

Dance of the Fractured Stars

Beneath the cosmos, the stars lose their way,
Fragmented dreams begin to sway.
A dance of light in a boundless sea,
Twirling through darkness, wild and free.

Each star a story, scattered and bright,
Whispers of magic in the still of night.
They pulse and shimmer, in a cosmic trance,
Inviting the lonely to join in the dance.

With every flicker, hope finds a spark,
In the fractured sky, there's beauty in dark.
Let the stars guide us through shadows and scars,
In the celestial ballet, we are all just stars.

Painting the Unsung Chaos

In the shadows where secrets dwell,
Colors clash and freely swell.
Brushes dance in wild delight,
Creating chaos, pure and bright.

The canvas holds the silent screams,
Where truth is lost in vibrant dreams.
Each stroke a heartbeat, raw and true,
In every hue, a tale is due.

From turmoil springs a vivid sight,
Emotions captured in the light.
The artist's hand wields joy and fear,
In unsung chaos, visions clear.

In layers deep, the stories hide,
With every blend, we turn the tide.
To paint the world in colors bold,
Is to embrace what we've been told.

The Paradox of Unraveled Plans

In silence fall the lonesome dreams,
What seems to be is never as it seems.
Plans laid out with threads of fate,
But life unravels, never straight.

A map is drawn, yet paths confuse,
Each twist and turn, we must peruse.
Desires pinned like fleeting stars,
Yet tangled in the cosmic wars.

With every choice a fork in time,
The fragile steps, a frantic climb.
Though journeys start with clear intent,
The heart's direction often bent.

Embrace the fault lines of your way,
For paradox brings light to gray.
In chaos found, a spark ignites,
Even in fear, there lie delights.

Whispers of the Unruly

In the night where shadows creep,
Quiet secrets begin to seep.
The whispers call, wild and free,
Stirring hearts in a fray of glee.

Voices dance on restless winds,
Tales of love and loss rescinds.
In every sigh, a world unfolds,
Unruly dreams that dare be told.

In laughter shared and tears of pain,
We find our solace in the rain.
The chaos churns, a sweet embrace,
With every whisper, we find our place.

Let not the rules dictate our song,
For harmony is where we belong.
In jubilant noise, our spirits soar,
With whispers of the unruly, forevermore.

Serendipity's Dilemma

A chance encounter, paths collide,
In fleeting moments, hearts abide.
The smiles exchanged, a spark ignites,
In serendipity, destiny lights.

Yet choices heavy, weigh us down,
In joy and doubt, we dance around.
A twist of fate, so bittersweet,
As dreams unfold, the heart skips beats.

To grasp the gift or let it flee,
In every chance, a mystery.
For serendipity's a fickle friend,
With turns that leave us to amend.

We wander lost yet wholly found,
In chaos, beauty's often crowned.
In dilemmas rich with silent grace,
We find our truth in time and space.

Woven in Whirlwind

In the storm's wild embrace, we dance,
Whispers of fate in a fleeting glance.
Threads of the night swirl and collide,
In the eye of chaos, we take pride.

Colors bleed through the fabric of time,
Twists of reality in. rhythm and rhyme.
Hearts beat steady amidst the fray,
Woven in whirlwind, we find our way.

Through thunder's roar and lightning's spark,
We carve our path from the shadows dark.
Unraveled moments, yet tightly bound,
In the tapestry of life, we are found.

With every turn in the tempest's tale,
We stand together, we shall not fail.
Hand in hand, we rise and soar,
Woven in whirlwind, forevermore.

The Tapestry of Tumult

Stitched with threads of strife and grace,
A vibrant dance in this crowded space.
Each knot a story, each tear a song,
In the tapestry of tumult, we belong.

Fingers trace paths of sorrow and joy,
In chaos, we find the heart of the boy.
Colors entwined in a daring embrace,
Every heart beats with unfaltering pace.

Though shadows loom and the night draws near,
A tapestry brightens, we have no fear.
From discordant notes, a melody grows,
In the fabric of life, the essence flows.

Weaving together our hopes and dreams,
In the heart of the storm, the future gleams.
Through tumult and trials, we shall thrive,
In this rich tapestry, we come alive.

When Chaos Spoke Softly

When chaos spoke softly, I paused to hear,
A whisper of truth amidst the fear.
In the stillness, a melody rang,
Of fragile peace, where the heart sang.

Echoes of reason danced in the night,
Guiding the lost to the flickering light.
In the storm's lullaby, I found my way,
When chaos spoke softly, I chose to stay.

Threads of emotion wove through the air,
Stories of courage, hearts laid bare.
With every word, a promise took flight,
In the silence, we forged our might.

When chaos embraced us, we learned to bend,
In the quiet moments, we found a friend.
With gentle hands, we sculpted our fate,
When chaos spoke softly, love was our gate.

A Serenade for the Unraveled

In the shadows, where dreams entwine,
A serenade plays, soft and divine.
Melodies wrapped in a gentle embrace,
For the unraveled hearts who seek their place.

With every note that falls to the ground,
Whispers of solace can be found.
In the fragments, beauty begins to rise,
A symphony of hope beneath the skies.

Though we may falter and come undone,
In the chaos, new stories are spun.
Each thread that breaks allows light to shine,
A serenade for those lost in time.

In the dance of shadows, we learn to sway,
Through the broken pieces, love finds a way.
Together we'll weave a brighter song,
For the unraveled, where we all belong.

Laughter in the Storm

Raindrops dance on my window,
Thunder rumbles a lively tune.
In chaos, joy takes its flight,
Finding warmth in the monsoon.

Smiling faces amidst the gray,
Children splash in puddles wide.
With laughter echoing all around,
We embrace the storm, joy our guide.

Lightning flashes, bright and bold,
Each strike sparks a fleeting cheer.
In the heart of each tempest's grasp,
Laughter rings, loud and clear.

Let the skies roar, let winds howl,
We stand together, brave and strong.
For in the storm, our hearts unite,
In laughter where we all belong.

Chords of Confusion

Notes collide in tangled air,
Melodies clash, a wild sound.
Every strum, a twist of fate,
In the chaos, lost we're found.

Beats would sway, then halt at once,
Rhythms shift like shifting sands.
In the discord, voices rise,
A harmony no one quite understands.

Fingers dance on strings of doubt,
Chasing echoes through the night.
In the mix of wrong and right,
Confusion breeds a strange delight.

Yet in this storm of aural clash,
Listen close, a truth might gleam.
For even in the mess we make,
Resides the beauty of a dream.

Beauty in the Bedlam

Amidst the chaos, a calm can bloom,
Whispers hidden in the noise.
In scattered moments, light breaks through,
Bringing forth the heart's true joys.

Shattered glass and laughter blend,
Colors whirl, a riotous dance.
In bedlam's arms, we find our peace,
Embracing life's chaotic chance.

Wildflowers in a cracked sidewalk,
Beauty flourishes, fierce and free.
In the mess, there lies a spark,
Painting hope for all to see.

So let the world spin in a quake,
And let the tides rise and fall.
In the madness, we discover grace,
And in the bedlam, we stand tall.

The Unruly Melody

A tune breaks free, wild and bold,
Notes that twist and turn away.
In the shadows, the music speaks,
Creating chaos within the play.

Strings are pulled taut, then snap, then soar,
Rhythms clash like stormy seas.
Out of control, we ride the wave,
Embracing our own harmonies.

From discord springs new songs to sing,
In the recklessness, freedom thrums.
With every note, we redefine,
The beauty of what chaos becomes.

So let the melody run amok,
With every misstep, learn to glide.
In the unruly, find your voice,
And in the wild, let dreams abide.

Revelry in Ruin

In shadows deep, the laughter rings,
Amidst the stones, a memory clings.
Beneath the stars, the whispers play,
A dance of ghosts in the fading day.

With every crack, a tale unfolds,
Of battles fought and dreams of old.
The echoes rise with every cheer,
In ruin's heart, we find no fear.

From dust we leap, to skies we toast,
To lost tomorrows, we raise a ghost.
In revelry, we seek the truth,
A fleeting glimpse of lost our youth.

So gather round, and hear the sound,
Of joy in places once profound.
In ruin's grasp, we find delight,
A hopeful spark in the silent night.

The Joys of Jumbled Journeys

Through winding paths, we wander free,
With hearts aglow, we seek the key.
Each step unknown beneath our feet,
Adventure calls in rhythms sweet.

With tangled trails, our stories blend,
In chaos made, we find a friend.
From every turn, a lesson learned,
In jumbled ways, our spirits burned.

Uncharted lands, the maps we break,
In every stumble, the smiles we make.
The joy is found not in the goal,
But in the journey that brims the soul.

So let us roam, with laughter bright,
Through days and nights, in pure delight.
In every twist, our paths align,
In jumbled journeys, joy we find.

The Art of Clashing Colors

In vivid hues, the canvas blooms,
A riot sings through shadowed rooms.
With strokes of chaos, beauty thrives,
In clashing colors, the spirit dives.

A dash of red, a splash of blue,
All mixed together, a world anew.
From discord comes a vibrant light,
In every clash, we feel the fight.

So brush away the lines of fate,
In every shade, we recreate.
With every hue, a story told,
The art of clashing, brave and bold.

Embrace the clash, the mess we make,
In every color, our hearts awake.
Through chaos shines a beauty rare,
In art of colors, we find our flair.

The Lattice of Life's Labyrinth

In twists and turns, the paths entwine,
Through every choice, the threads align.
A lattice formed of dreams and fears,
In life's labyrinth, we shed our tears.

With shadows cast and lights that gleam,
We navigate the woven dream.
Each junction holds a chance to grow,
In tangled ways, our spirits flow.

As we wander through each maze,
In every corner, a truth displays.
The lessons learned from every fold,
In lattice work, our lives unfold.

So trust the paths that lead you on,
Through life's vast web, from dusk till dawn.
Embrace the twists, the turns, the strife,
In the labyrinth lies the art of life.

Echoes of an Untamed Mind

In shadows deep, a whisper stirs,
Thoughts collide like wildest furs,
Dreams take flight on spectral wings,
Free and fierce as silence sings.

Untamed roars in fragile night,
Visions dance in flickering light,
Chaos spins a tangled thread,
Woven tales of lives unsaid.

Amidst the storm, a steady beat,
Pulse of spirit, fierce and sweet,
Echoes linger, drift, and twist,
In the heart, they can't be missed.

A mind unleashed, so wild and vast,
In every thought, a thunderous cast,
With every echo, truths rewind,
Embrace the echoes, dear untamed mind.

The Beauty of Broken Pathways

Cracks in stone, a story told,
Where dreams once grew, now stand so bold,
Beauty lies in what has frayed,
In every step, a love displayed.

Worn-out soles on jagged ways,
Lead to lights of brighter days,
Through the pain, we learn to see,
The grace of life, the art to be.

Each turn and twist, a memory bright,
Reflections catch the fading light,
A tapestry of hopes and fears,
Weaving love through laughter and tears.

Broken pathways, though they twist,
Invite us to a timeless tryst,
In every fracture, beauty shines,
A journey marked by love's designs.

Whirlwinds of Intention

Spirals spin in unseen play,
Intentions float on winds of way,
Hearts align in cosmic dance,
A whirlwind's stir, a fleeting chance.

In currents strong, our dreams we cast,
With whispers soft, our shadows last,
In every turn, a thought takes flight,
Whirlwinds sweep us into the night.

Purpose flows like rivers wide,
Guiding us on this wild ride,
Bound by hope, unchained we fly,
Through tempests fierce, we learn to try.

With focus sharp, we break the air,
Crafting dreams with subtle care,
In whirlwinds bold, we find our way,
Breath of intention leads the day.

Finding Grace in the Unruly

In chaos vast, we search for peace,
A gentle heart, our sweet release,
Among the wild, a truth unfolds,
Grace blooms bright where chaos molds.

Through tangled vines and storms that roar,
We learn to walk the rugged floor,
With every fall, a lesson found,
In unruly dance, our souls are bound.

The beauty of the flawed and free,
Unfolds in ways we yearn to see,
With open arms, we face the night,
Finding grace in every fight.

So let the world spin round and round,
In life's embrace, true hope is found,
In every chaos, we discern,
That grace will bloom, and hearts will yearn.

The Art of Beautiful Disorder

In tangled threads of fate we weave,
Chaos whispers sweet reprieve.
The dance of life, a wild spree,
In disarray, we find our glee.

Colors clash in vivid hues,
Melodies born from scattered cues.
In every flaw, a story's told,
In rough edges, joys unfold.

The heart beats loud in broken time,
In each misstep, we learn to rhyme.
Embrace the mess, let shadows play,
For beauty blooms in disarray.

With open arms, we dare to dream,
In every scream, a silent gleam.
The art we make, a sweet divorce,
From perfect lines to radiant course.

Fate's Playful Hand

A shuffle of cards, the game begins,
In laughter and chance, fortune spins.
With every roll, a new path's laid,
In fate's embrace, we're unafraid.

The moon winks at lovers below,
As stars dance in a cosmic flow.
With hands entwined, the moment shares,
The playful tease of fate declares.

Life's a canvas, bright and bold,
Where stories of hearts are gently told.
In twists and turns, we find our place,
In fate's warm hand, we float with grace.

Together we carve the unknown trail,
With whispers soft, we set the sail.
For in this journey, hand in hand,
We brave the whims of fate's command.

Anarchy's Embrace

In shadowed streets where silence brews,
Anarchy blooms in vibrant hues.
With every shout, a spirit rises,
In the chaos, truth disguises.

The rules are broken, lines erased,
In freedom's kiss, we find our taste.
With hearts ablaze, we join the fray,
In discord's arms, we choose to stay.

The siren's call, it pulls us tight,
A rebel's hymn in the dead of night.
For in the wild, we find our song,
In the storm, we feel so strong.

Embrace the fight, let voices soar,
In harmony found on the battleground floor.
In anarchy's cradle, we make our stand,
With open hearts and a steady hand.

The Crescendo of Clatter

In the din of life, a symphony plays,
With every clash, it softly sways.
From pots and pans, a rhythm grows,
In loud embraces, pure joy flows.

Footsteps echo on cobblestone,
As laughter rings, the night's our own.
With jumbled voices, we weave our song,
In the heart of noise, we all belong.

The world awakens, vibrant and bright,
Each crack, each clash, ignites the night.
In the chaos, a beauty stirs,
A dance of souls, in softest purrs.

Let the clatter rise, let spirits soar,
In every note, we crave for more.
For in the crescendo, we find our way,
In the pulse of life, we laugh and play.

A Serenade for the Uncoordinated

In a dance of missteps bright,
Two left feet in borrowed light.
Laughing in a clumsy whirl,
Falling for a fleeting girl.

Every twirl a hapless drift,
Yet there's joy in each small shift.
Eyes that sparkle, hearts that race,
Finding rhythm in the space.

Laughter echoes in the air,
As they trip without a care.
Casting shadows, light takes flight,
In their chaos, pure delight.

So here's to those who dare to sway,
In a world that leads astray.
With each stumble, love's refrain,
A serenade for joy or pain.

The Radiance of Ruin

Amidst the ashes, embers glow,
A beauty found in sorrow's flow.
Crumbled walls and shattered dreams,
Whisper tales of brighter themes.

A haunting grace in every scar,
Each fragment shines, a gleaming star.
Through broken glass, the light still breaks,
A path emerges, hope awakes.

In decay, a promise lies,
New beginnings mask goodbyes.
From shadows deep, the dawn will rise,
Transforming ruins into skies.

The radiance sings through despair,
We find our strength, and we repair.
A dance of life, the cycle spins,
From every end, the new begins.

In the Midst of the Spiral

Winding paths that twist and turn,
Lessons held, the heart will learn.
In the chaos, patterns spin,
A journey found from deep within.

Each curve a moment, fleeting, bright,
A glimpse of truth, a dance of light.
Stars align in grand design,
In the spiral, all is divine.

Step by step, we chase the dream,
Flowing as a gentle stream.
Time unfolds in vivid hues,
In the depths, we find our cues.

In the midst, we pause and see,
What once was lost can set us free.
Life's a cycle, ever real,
A spiral song, our hearts reveal.

Whispers from the Maelstrom

In the tempest, voices tease,
Caught in currents, aim to please.
Echoes blend in frantic flight,
A symphony in darkest night.

Secrets swirl where shadows play,
Tales of hope lost along the way.
Yet amidst the swirling storm,
A quiet peace begins to form.

From chaos springs a silver thread,
Whispers soft where fears have fled.
Guiding hearts through restless tides,
Finding calm where chaos hides.

Listen close, the winds will share,
Voices true, a calming prayer.
In the maelstrom, strength will gleam,
Whispers weave a brighter dream.

Rebellion in a Quiet Room

Silent screams may fill the air,
Shadows dance in muted glare.
Thoughts collide without a sound,
Hidden truths in chaos found.

Walls that cage the restless mind,
Boundless dreams we seek to find.
With each breath, we break the norm,
In stillness, we unleash the storm.

Fingers trace the edge of fate,
In secret corners, hearts debate.
Rebellion sparks in whispered tones,
A quiet roar, a heart that groans.

Voices echo, soft yet loud,
In silence, we are fierce and proud.
In this room, our spirits soar,
A gentle war, forevermore.

Ode to Unpredictable Freedom

Winds of chance, they twist and twirl,
Life's a dance, a fleeting whirl.
Roads unknown, we take the leap,
In chaotic paths, our souls we keep.

Freedom calls, a siren's song,
In its grasp, we all belong.
Moments wild, unplanned delight,
Stars that shine on paths of night.

Time unraveled, a vibrant thread,
Each mistake, a step ahead.
In every turn, we find surprise,
With open hearts, we learn to rise.

Courage blooms in uncertain air,
Living wild, without a care.
Unpredictable, sweet and bright,
Freedom dances in the light.

Embracing the Beautiful Disorder

Life's a tapestry, threads askew,
Colors blend in a messy hue.
Chaos whispers, sweet and loud,
In the fray, we stand unbowed.

Nature's symphony, wild and free,
Each note rings with fateful glee.
From tangled roots, our dreams arise,
In disorder's arms, we find the skies.

Embrace the flaws, the crooked bends,
In every twist, a story sends.
Beauty lies in the unrefined,
In every heart, a truth defined.

Through cracked surfaces, light can stream,
In beautiful chaos, we dare to dream.
With open arms, we greet the mess,
In every stumble, we find our bless.

The Art of Tangled Dreams

Whispers weave in silver threads,
Dreams entwined, where courage treads.
Glimmers bright in shadows roam,
In tangled hopes, we find our home.

Each knot a wish, each loop a sigh,
In vibrant colors, we learn to fly.
Stories dance on the edge of night,
In dreamer's hearts, we find our light.

We draw with stars upon the skin,
Chasing stories, where we begin.
In perfect flaws, our visions gleam,
With every heartbeat, live the dream.

Tangled threads that bind us tight,
We savor chaos, embrace the night.
In the art of dreams, we weave our fate,
Together we rise, never too late.

The Mosaic of Mayhem

Colors clash in vivid hues,
Chaos dances, an endless muse.
Fragments scattered, tales unfold,
In this madness, beauty bold.

Voices rise like tempests strong,
Notes of life, a wild song.
Shapes and shadows intertwine,
In this chaos, we define.

Every piece, a story told,
In the mayhem, hearts turn gold.
Weaving dreams, a vibrant thread,
In the frenzy, we are led.

Amidst the storm, a calm we find,
In the chaos, love is blind.
A mosaic crafted, rich and bright,
In the mayhem, we find light.

Serene Turbulence

Waves crash gently on the shore,
Whispers echo, forevermore.
The sun dips low, a golden glow,
In the stillness, currents flow.

Clouds drift by, a soft ballet,
In the chaos, peace will stay.
Hearts entwined in subtle grace,
Finding beauty in this space.

Ripples dance, the breeze in tune,
Beneath the tempest, stars are strewn.
Through storms we sail, unbroken dreams,
In turbulence, life redeems.

Serene rhythms guide our way,
In the turmoil, hope will play.
Balance found in nature's rhyme,
Turbulence embraced, sublime.

Contradictions in Bloom

Petals soft, thorns beneath,
Beauty hides, a complex sheath.
Joy and sorrow intertwined,
In the garden, truth we find.

Sunshine breaks, the shadows fall,
Hope can rise amidst it all.
Tears may water roots so deep,
In this contrast, secrets keep.

Colors clash, a vibrant shout,
Life blooms loud, there's no doubt.
Every struggle, every pain,
Sprouts the beauty we attain.

In the chaos, love will sprout,
Contradictions weave about.
From the darkness, light shall bloom,
In each heart, dispel the gloom.

The Poetry of Pandemonium

A dance of chaos, wild and free,
Words collide in symphony.
Voices clash, a fervent roar,
In this pandemonium, hearts explore.

Pens on fire, ink takes flight,
Stories thrumming, day and night.
In the whirlwind, truth ignites,
From the chaos, wisdom bites.

Rhyme and reason, out of sync,
In this fray, we dare to think.
Every madness holds a spark,
In the shadows, we leave our mark.

Beauty found in the disorder,
Words like waves, bend and border.
In the tumult, voices blend,
The poetry of life, no end.

Graceful Missteps

In shadows cast by chance we dance,
Our feet may stumble, yet we prance.
With every fall, we rise anew,
A symphony of grace in each view.

Through tangled paths, our hearts entwine,
Mistakes may guide, in ways divine.
Each step a note in life's sweet song,
A testament that we belong.

In whispered doubts, we find our strength,
Embrace the journey, at arm's length.
The beauty lies in every turn,
In missteps made, our spirits burn.

So let us waltz through veiled unknowns,
With open hearts, we'll find our homes.
For in this dance of fate and trust,
All graceful missteps turn to dust.

Fraying Threads of Destiny

In twilight's glow, the fabric frays,
Threads of fate in delicate haze.
Each stitch a choice, a path unknown,
Woven dreams in twilight grown.

Beneath the stars, our stories intertwine,
A tapestry of moments divine.
Yet with each pull, the pattern shifts,
In shadows cast, the heart still lifts.

We gather hope from tangled strands,
In hands of fate, we weave our plans.
Though chaos reigns, the beauty stays,
In every fray, our souls ablaze.

So let us cherish this fragile art,
For destiny's hand guides every heart.
In threads once torn, new colors flow,
Fraying threads beget the glow.

The Allure of the Unexpected

In moments fleeting, surprises gleam,
The world unfolds like a waking dream.
With every turn, a fresh delight,
Uncharted paths in the soft twilight.

A whispered breeze, a gentle sigh,
The beauty found in the passing by.
In laughter shared and smiles awoken,
In words unspoken, bonds unbroken.

So venture forth where shadows play,
In the allure of night and day.
Embrace the twists, the turns, the bends,
For life reveals what never ends.

With arms wide open, let us dare,
To find the magic lingering there.
In every chance, let wonder thrive,
The unexpected keeps us alive.

Jigsaw of Jumbled Dreams

In pieces scattered, a puzzle waits,
Where hopes collide and love creates.
Each fragment holds a tale to tell,
In jigsaw dreams, we weave our spell.

With colors bright and shadows deep,
In every corner, our secrets keep.
The edges rough, yet hearts align,
In chaos found, our paths define.

Through trials faced, we fit the parts,
In every challenge, we find our hearts.
With patience born from time's embrace,
We find our place in this vast space.

So let us gather, piece by piece,
In this grand mosaic, a sweet release.
For in the blend of dreams we find,
A portrait of the intertwined.

The Harmony of Hiccups

In the quiet of the night, they rise,
Little bursts like secret sighs.
A melody of laughter breaks,
Sweet reminders of the stakes.

Each hiccup brings a pause to time,
A rhythm that is simply sublime.
They dance between each breath we take,
In playful moments, smiles awake.

With gentle chaos, we find our way,
In the hilarity of the day.
A chorus sung in fits and starts,
Echoing through our joyful hearts.

So let them come, these tiny tunes,
Underneath the laughing moons.
For in their fleeting, silly grace,
We find our peace, we find our place.

Twists and Turns of Fate

Paths we wander, lost and found,
Winding trails on shaky ground.
Each step leads to what awaits,
In the maze of twisted fates.

Moments shift like desert sands,
Plans drawn clear slip through our hands.
What's meant to be, can't be restrained,
In the dance of joy and pain.

Choices echo, shadows call,
With every rise, there comes a fall.
Yet through the trials, we remain,
Woven tight in joy and strain.

So here we stand, both brave and bold,
In every story yet untold.
Embracing all that life bestows,
Through twists and turns, our spirit grows.

Dance of the Disordered

In the whirl of life's great cha-cha,
Steps are messy, oh, hurrah!
Figures flail, but hearts stay light,
Lost in the music of the night.

Spinning, twirling, laughter's spark,
Shadows creep along the park.
Each misstep holds a chance to feel,
The joy in chaos, raw and real.

Fingers clasped, we wade through chance,
In a disordered, wild dance.
We are the makers of our art,
Each stumble beats within the heart.

So join the fray, don't walk away,
Find the rhythm, come what may.
In every swirl, we find the bliss,
In disarray, there's nothing amiss.

Chaos as Canvas

Splashes bright on blank white space,
Colors clash, yet find their place.
In the chaos, beauty grows,
Each stroke tells what nobody knows.

With frantic brush and fleeting glance,
We create the dreamers' dance.
Lines and forms, a wild embrace,
Captured in this crazy race.

Brush against the edges, bold,
Stories of mystery unfold.
Chaos paints a vivid scene,
In every clash, the unseen sheen.

So let the mess be part of art,
In every swirl, we pour our heart.
For out of chaos, life will rise,
A masterpiece beneath the skies.

Paradox of the Unplanned

In chaos, we find our plans,
As life dances with unseen hands.
Unraveled dreams scatter like dust,
Yet in their midst, we learn to trust.

Through tangled roots, our paths entwine,
Mistakes become the sweetest wine.
The map we draw fades in the night,
For in the dark, we find our light.

Waves crash down, yet we float free,
In storms, we learn who we can be.
A step unplanned, the leap of faith,
In every stumble, we find grace.

What's left unspoken, fills the air,
In silence, we mend every tear.
The paradox is where we stand,
In not knowing, we take our hand.

The Sweetness of the Wild

In the thicket, whispers sigh,
Wildflowers bloom, colors apply.
The fragrance lingers in the breeze,
Nature's song brings hearts to ease.

Beneath the boughs, a secret tune,
The dance of dusk, the rise of moon.
Crickets chirp in joyful play,
Life bursts forth, come what may.

Freedom dwells where rivers roam,
In wildness, we find our home.
Every rustle, a tale to tell,
In whispered winds, our spirits dwell.

Sweet moments in untamed places,
Life unfurls in gentle traces.
In the wildness, souls take flight,
Find the sweetness in the night.

Echoes of Entangled Paths

Across the years, our stories bind,
Threads of fate, we're intertwined.
Lost in laughter, found in tears,
We walk together, despite our fears.

Footsteps echo through the mist,
In every meeting, fate's sweet kiss.
Unseen forces draw us near,
In every joy, in every fear.

A glance exchanged, a moment shared,
In tangled lives, we are ensnared.
The paths we tread, a winding course,
In every turn, we find the force.

Through valleys deep and mountains high,
We seek the truth, we reach the sky.
The echoes last, though time moves on,
In shared heartbeats, we are strong.

The Joy of the Chaotic Heart

In currents swift, my heart does race,
An untamed spirit finds its place.
Through storms of life, I dance and spin,
In chaos, I find the joy within.

Each heartbeat sings a wild refrain,
Amidst the chaos, I shed the pain.
With every stumble, I rise anew,
In the tumult, I find my view.

Passions flare like fire's gleam,
In chaos, I live my fiercest dream.
Let the world whirl in disarray,
For in the chaos, I choose to stay.

A symphony of love and strife,
In every clash, I find my life.
Embrace the wild, the messy part,
In every challenge, beats my heart.

Milton Keynes UK
Ingram Content Group UK Ltd.
UKHW031319271124
451618UK00007B/227